To My Mother

Letters She'll Never Read

Kara Almonte

India | USA | UK

Copyright © Kara Almonte
All Rights Reserved.

This book has been self-published with all reasonable efforts taken to make the material error-free by the author. No part of this book shall be used, reproduced in any manner whatsoever without written permission from the author, except in the case of brief quotations embodied in critical articles and reviews.

The Author of this book is solely responsible and liable for its content including but not limited to the views, representations, descriptions, statements, information, opinions, and references ["Content"]. The Content of this book shall not constitute or be construed or deemed to reflect the opinion or expression of the Publisher or Editor. Neither the Publisher nor Editor endorse or approve the Content of this book or guarantee the reliability, accuracy, or completeness of the Content published herein and do not make any representations or warranties of any kind, express or implied, including but not limited to the implied warranties of merchantability, fitness for a particular purpose.

The Publisher and Editor shall not be liable whatsoever...

Made with ❤ on the BookLeaf Publishing Platform
www.bookleafpub.in
www.bookleafpub.com

Dedication

For my inner child, who will always long for a Mom

Preface

These pages serve as my catharsis and final stage of letting go. For anyone who has not had a loving relationship with their mother, I hope this book helps you to know that you are not alone. We all have to find our way in this world, but it all starts with our mothers. The people we are born from set our trajectory in ways we don't even realize, but how we steer our direction is what will determine where life takes us. It's our parents' first time living too, and I can truly empathize with that. This book is not meant to degrade my mother, however, I am genuinely sharing my own experiences. The purpose of this is to leave my grievances on these pages so that I may no longer feel the weight of carrying these things in my heart. I hope that it can inspire others to find their own ways to put down their burdens as well and carry on their path with love and light. We don't always get to say these things to the people who should hear them, but they should be said nonetheless.

Acknowledgements

Thank you to my sister.
For your guidance, discipline and love.

Wishes

I wish we could have been friends
Like all the girls I've encountered
Who said their best friends were their mothers
Who said they couldn't imagine a life without them
I wish that you had loved me
The way a mother should love a daughter
Nurturing and kind
Patient and encouraging
I wish your mother had loved you
So that you would know how to love
I wish she raised you better
And taught you right from wrong
I wish I wasn't ashamed of you
For everything you are
To carry this resentment
Is a taxing endeavor
I wish I could forget
All the damage you've done
Because forgiveness is easy
But forgetting is the hard part
I wish you could be happy
I wish that you knew me
But wishes are for shooting stars
And all I've ever known is darkness

Worlds

The world that you raised me in
The one that I knew
Was a world away
From which you came
Oceans and land masses apart
You were the snowbird
And he was the root
Of course
This is paradise
Many have made the journey
To bask on these shores
Yourself included
It's nothing new
Offered nothing of substance
Your beak was always too high
When in fact
You couldn't even fly
That's how the root got you
Low hanging fruit
Is always the first to go
But you were already on the ground
Rotting flesh
The root deserved better

You weren't the first pick
But the root was broken too

You

It was always about you
Not a moment went by
Where you couldn't focus
On anything but yourself
The center of the universe
You'd always say
The world doesn't revolve around you
But for you it did
It was out to get you
Nothing in your favor
But enemies at every turn
It never occurred to you
The enemy was you
No one was safe
From your anger
From your revenge
Their innocence
Their good intentions
None of it mattered
They were in cahoots
They had it out for you
Your delusions
Made everyone evil

Kindness didn't exist in your world
Unless you needed it

Why

Sometimes I wonder
Why did you have kids?
Did you even want them?
Beyond having someone to love you
Beyond trying to fill the hole in your heart
Did you want us to be happy?
Or were you just checking off the list?
Get married
Have kids
Have a house
Was it all a lie?
Did you even want to be there?
What was the point?
To never have to work again?
To pretend that you were a parent?
I have so many questions
And so little answers
The liar in you would never tell
Even if I dared to ask
Honestly
I don't even think you know
Why you did the things you did
I don't think you'll ever know
What you were doing

And so will I
Never know
Why

Blind

You never really had any friends
To this day
You still don't
Maybe one
But not really
To have a friend
Is to be a friend
Something you never understood
Something you could never execute
Being kind
Being selfless
Being caring
Doing things when it's inconvenient
Being there when it's hard
Having fights
Saying you're sorry
You never could apologize
Even when you were wrong
Even when you knew you should
Which wasn't very often
But even then
You'd shut down
Pretend like nothing happened
No one was ever good enough

No one was better than you
No one was deserving
The projections you'd make
Could fill an entire stadium
Blinding lights
That you would never see
You keep your eyes closed
But fail to look within

Seesaw

I can still remember the seesaw
Up and down we'd go
Some days were good
But the episodes
Took a toll
The fights were often
The flees were imminent
Sometimes you'd take me with you
Most days you'd leave me behind
But always to return
And threaten again
That our whole world
Hung in the balance
Every day
We walked on eggshells
Tip toed around you
Your favorite threat was suicide
I learned that very early
Anything could be a weapon
The car we drove to school
A kitchen knife that made dinner
The gun hidden under the bed
The fragility of it all
As he told me to dial

Call 911 he'd say
As I stood there frozen
Merely a child
How could I know
The things that I'd witness
Would impress on me
So deeply

Singles

It's a strange profession
One as old as time
In one form or another
You were never shy
I would try on your shoes
Try to balance on them like stilts
With the other little girls
Whose mothers were like you
I guess I can see the appeal
I've heard it can be hard
To get a normal job
Once you've had a taste
You'd come home at sunrise
And let me count the ones
The smell of dirty money
Reminds me of you
You kept them in your little red purse
Dumped them onto the floor
And uncrumpled the dollars
I'd put them up to my face
I always liked the smell
And when you'd leave at night
I would cry
Awaiting your return

To hug me
And let me count the money
With you

Scene

When you first had me
I was like a puppy
You thought I was cute
And showed me off to the world
Then I got older
And the novelty faded
I became too much work
Parties were more fun for you
But you managed to drag me along
Adults always around
Rarely other children
Bedtimes didn't exist
We went where you wanted
And did what you liked
I was just along for the ride
A very long bumpy ride
The people spoke gibberish
While you spread yourself around
Far and wide we went
The many men I met
They were all the same
You wanted to play
But I was your alibi
Your confidant

It wasn't fair
Though life rarely is
Doomed at conception
I was just a kid

Frozen

I can't remember many moments of peace
That's the thing with memories
We can block them out
If it hurts too much
Or if they make us too sad
We forget it in a sense
But not really
The memory stays in us
Locked away deep inside
The darkest corners of our minds
Where we bury the pain
That would break us
If we faced it
The memories that would send us
Straight over the cliff
And take all our sanity with them
Do not mistake me
There were some good times
But few and far between
Never without a touch of fear
A spout of anger
An outburst
My memories are flooded
With moments like this

Insecurity
Instability
Danger
Forever stuck
In survival mode
Unable to reminisce
The darkness lingers
Triggered
I exist

To Be

It was the aching need for attention
It was the desperation
The absolute self loathing
The need for validation
From anyone
For anything
It shaped your life
It made you who you are
Your entire personality
Was molded around it
Who are you really?
Underneath the narcissist
Beneath the inflated ego
Is it just your self pity?
Is your entitlement also there?
Sometimes I feel bad for you
And other times I remember
Remember the hurt
Remember the malice
The phone calls you made
The houses you'd stalk
The people you threatened
The lies that you spread
And for what?

The need for control
The claws that dug in
Clutching into me
Chasing me through the street
Choking me on the grate
Slandering your child
You would believe your own lies
Before you ever believed
In the good in me
When all I ever wanted
Was to feel safe
To feel loved
To feel seen
What a daughter I could have been

Neck

I can still remember flashes
Bits and pieces
Of here and there
Nothing truly concrete
My memories are spotty
It was a birthday
A pool party
I was rarely invited to things like that
And if I was
I couldn't go without you
I was nine
Awkward at best
As I stood there quietly
You chattered up the room
Uncomfortable
I think we all were
You pushed me in the pool
And then another child
And then another
There I was
At the bottom
Swimming up for air
When two feet struck me
Straight on the head

I could hear the crunch
Feel the sharp pain
Shooting up my spine
As I struggled to swim
Back up for air
I gasped
In shock
Flailing
Choking
Reaching for the edge
I felt the pull
Someone else came to my rescue
As you continued on
Without a care in the world
My neck still hurts

Cat and Mouse

My first attempt was five
Maybe six
I packed two plastic bags
One on each handle bar
I made it to the corner of the street
A whole 10 seconds away
I sat there on the ground
As the cars passed
Staring at the house
Waiting for you to come
Some time went by
I can't recall exactly how much
Enough for a neighbor to come out
And take me back home
There was another attempt
Some years later
One night at the ranch
You'd had some drinks
Smoked some weed
I was your easy target
Keeping you entertained
Tears ran down my face
I walked out the door
Into the pitch black

Barefoot on the red dirt
I made it 20 paces or so
And turned around
To aloneness
More years went by
The screaming was unbearable
I'd take long walks in the dark
To a place that was safe
I was twelve
You'd found me and took me back
To that volatile house
Then finally fifteen
Big enough to go the distance
You were relentless
In your pursuit
For the teenager
Who was searching for safety
But for all those years
That little girl
Was not worth chasing

Wonder

I'll admit
I wasn't perfect
Troubled as any young girl
Without any guidance
Without a role model
Without support
Often I wonder
Who I would have been
Had there been discipline
Had there been concern
Had there been care
Where would I be
If you'd driven me to practice
Asked me about my homework
Packed my lunches
Helped me with my science project
Brushed my hair on picture day
Made home cooked meals
But there was always something
More pressing
More important
More paramount
For you to tend to
Whether it was parties

Or getting your degree
Or going back to work at the clubs
Or any of the failed businesses
Or any of the countless affairs
Or causing destruction
How could I ever be perfect
How could I be any semblance of good
When I was a product of you

Trip

Our first and only trip together
Was to California
I'd never left home before
So far isolated in the Pacific
You'd always talk about Michigan
About the cold winters in Detroit
Till this day I still haven't been
But back then
I was so excited
To venture out of our little corner of the world
I was twelve
You told me we were taking the dog
Across the ocean to my half sister
A "mother daughter trip"
A visit to my sister in college
Quality time together
But that wasn't it at all
You could have shipped the dog
But I was your alibi
It made a great cover up
Almost believable you'd want to do that
For the step child you loathed so badly
I was rarely allowed to see her
So I thought it was such a treat

I only saw her once that week
We spent a majority of the time with him
He was from Australia
We stayed in a cheap motel
And went to the Santa Monica Pier
He took us on rides
And as we sped through the air
I wondered why we were here
Spending time with this strange man
Then when the sky got dark
You'd leave me at the motel
I'd watch tv and eat junk food
And when you returned
You'd chat me up like a peer
I was so numb
But I still remember your rage
When I outed you a few years later
I was never sure if he knew
Or if I should say anything at all
Dad looked so broken

Role Model

Your love was free
Open to anyone
Like a flower
You'd take any bee
Among other drugs
Attention was the best high
Validation was an addiction
You modeled it for me
To be unyielding
In the pursuit of affection
Regardless of the source
Or the intentions
A fleeting moment
Was better than nothing
To be alone
Was worse than being used
It's no surprise
I was just as bad as you
Everyone said
I'd follow your footsteps
And so I became
A self fulfilling prophecy
I told myself
If people think that I'm bad

I may as well have fun
But no one tells you
That kind of shame
It stays with you
You never quite live it down
No matter how many years pass
Or how much you accomplish
The success you create
Is never as memorable
As your mistakes

Missed

I can still smell the dried up cereal
The mold of the milk under the newspaper
You never taught me how to clean
You couldn't teach me
What you didn't know
I'd sleep on the couch
And eat on the bed
The tv was my only friend
You kept me inside
Isolated from the world
I'd flip the mop upside down
And pretend
You played with me a lot when I was little
Then resented me as I grew
You saw me as competition
Any female was a threat
That I knew
I learned to make myself small
To be quiet
To please you
But you were insatiable
The rules never made sense
It was lonely
But I learned to enjoy the solitude

Now it's being around you that's hard
I don't miss you
And it makes me sad
Because I wish that I did
While you're alive
I'll learn to grieve you

Jump

When I was fifteen
I really didn't care about anything
I didn't have any goals
Except to be anywhere but here
To feel safe or feel nothing at all
I fell into the trap
I opted to feel nothing
It was the easier option
When you have little to no resources
You learn to be resourceful
When you're a girl in particular
You find ways to get things
Men were easy like that
But I'd managed to find others
Just like me
Who didn't want to feel
One day I came back
You had assumptions
About what I'd been doing
None of them true
Right then you decided
You needed to pull in my reins
But I was untamable
I'd been neglected so long

I never thought you would care
But it wasn't concern
It was control
I jumped out the second story window
And ran through the drive
You caught me at the road
And put me in a chokehold
Dad yelled at you to let me go
I broke free
And sprinted into the dark
Barefoot
Past the police car
Around the corner
I jumped into a ditch
And I laid there
As they circled the block
I waited patiently
Until my getaway car arrived
Parked across the street
Waiting for me at the beach
I timed it perfectly
And ran to freedom
That was the last time
You would ever try to control me
Everything after that
Was my choice
I was liberated

Villain

It wasn't until my early twenties
I'd confided in someone
She told me to forgive you
Not for your sake
But for mine
That I'd never be healed
Until I let it all go
There was so much rage
So much pain inside me
I carried it around
And I couldn't figure out
How to put it down
I'd take long walks
Through the mountains
While shedding tears
And repeated to myself
"I forgive you"
It took everything I had
To make myself believe those words
Now I am thirty
And I still wonder if I do
Truly forgive you
I know that I want to
To believe you didn't know any better

That you weren't capable
That you aren't culpable
For all the damage
That I must undo
Because of you
Even still
My blood starts to boil
When you're around me
When you try to hug me
Or act like you care
Because in my story
You will always be the villain

Cheers

There's a saying
If a flower doesn't bloom
You change its environment
Now more than ever
Have I bloomed
Finally do I feel
Like I am thriving
And yet
As of late
I've attended weddings
To always find myself
Tearing up
When the parents of the bride
Shower their daughter
In beautiful speeches
With love and support
To usher her into the next phase
Wishing her love
Wishing her happiness
Lending their wisdom
I pretend they're happy tears
But deep down I know
I'll never have that
And it's an aching pain

That I've learned to accept
And I am happy for those
Who have mothers
That celebrate their daughters
At the same time
I am filled with envy
And resentment
For my mentally unstable mother
For my emotionally absent father
And I tell myself
"It could be worse"
As I quietly wipe my tears
And take another sip of champagne
Awaiting to cheers
The happy couple

Access

It has been said
That absence makes the heart grow fonder
I don't know if that's true
Now that absence is my favorite part of you
You call me
But I don't answer
Leave messages
That I don't return
Crumbs of information
About what I'm up to
Is all you get now
Being able to choose
How much access you get to me
Is my greatest superpower
Your insincerity unconcealed
I hear it in your voice
The way your words get higher
"I'm glad you're having so much fun"
Are you?
Being happy for other people
Was never your forte
And I find it so strange
How even now
The sound of your voice

Grinds something inside me
Like a knife to the pavement
Scratching along
I cringe at the thought
Of having to see you again
And I hope that I don't have to
Please don't get me wrong
People always say
"But she's your mother"
It's just that she never was
Truly a mother
To me

Me

You never saw me
As an individual
But as an extension
Of yourself
It's funny how that works
In your mind
If I was bad
I was possessed by evil
Infected with the devil
On the other hand
If I was good
Accomplished
It was a credit to you
A reflection of you
Such a parallel
But when you think about it
Really
Two sides of the same coin
Either way you flip it
There you are
But I'm not you
And as much as you'd like to take credit
For the roses that I've grown
While deflecting all of my thorns

This will always be my garden
You gave me a seed
But it was me
Who worked the soil
Found the sunshine
And waited out the rains
Make no mistake
This is me

www.ingramcontent.com/pod-product-compliance
Lightning Source LLC
Chambersburg PA
CBHW070039070426
42449CB00012BA/3105